How to Make the Best
of Sibling Rivalry

CHARLES FAY, PH.D.

How to Make the Best of Sibling Rivalry

CHARLES FAY, PH.D.

The Love and Logic® PRESS Inc.

Love and Logic Press, Inc.

2207 Jackson Street, Golden, CO 80401-2300

www.loveandlogic.com

800-338-4065

LOVE AND LOGIC, LOVE & LOGIC, BECOMING A LOVE AND LOGIC PARENT, AMERICA'S PARENTING EXPERTS, LOVE AND LOGIC MAGIC, 9 ESSENTIAL SKILLS FOR THE LOVE AND LOGIC CLASSROOM, and are registered trademarks or trademarks of the Institute For Professional Development, Ltd. and may not be used without written permission expressly granted from the Institute For Professional Development, Ltd.

Library of Congress Cataloging-in-Publication Data

Fay, Charles, 1964-
 How to make the best of sibling rivalry : as seen on public television /
Charles Fay, Ph.D.
    p. cm.
 Includes bibliographical references and index.
 ISBN 978-1-930429-98-7 (pbk. : alk. paper)
 1. Sibling rivalry. 2. Parenting--Psychological aspects. I. Title.
 BF723.S43F38 2008
 649'.143--dc22
                    2008042745

Published and printed in the United States of America

TABLE OF CONTENTS

ACKNOWLEDGMENTS

This book wouldn't be written if it weren't for the great creativity, hard work, and love of two men. One is my father, Jim Fay. Despite the fact that he started his parenting life making plenty of mistakes with my two sisters and I, he loved us enough to keep learning and improving. Through his work as a school teacher and administrator, he began to recognize that there is no more precious gift we can give our kids than the ability to behave respectfully and responsibly. After extensive research and in-the-trenches experience, he began to develop a theory and set of techniques for helping parents give this gift.

When he met Foster W. Cline, M.D., the creative sparks really began to fly! Like two little kids discovering the only mud puddle on the playground, they couldn't help but jump right in. My father discovered that Foster is a wise and brilliant man. Even more importantly, we all discovered that Foster is a fine man filled with great character and love. His experience as a child psychiatrist—as well as his extreme sense of humor—were just what was needed! Through their creative partnership, they developed what the world now knows as Love and Logic.

Thanks also to my two wonderful sisters, Susie and Nancy. If it weren't for them, I would have spent my childhood looking for someone to annoy. Although they certainly lost their tempers with me from time to time, the degree of grace they showed their little brother is probably beyond comprehension. From them I learned many things—each of which I am extremely grateful.

MOST IMPORTANTLY, thanks to all of the patient mothers in the world who do the hard work—day in and day out—with little or no recognition. Without my mother, Shirley, my father would have never achieved what he has. Without his wife, Hermie, Foster would be lost. Without my wonderful wife, Monica, I wouldn't have a clue.

Moms of the world we love you!

ABOUT THE AUTHOR

Dr. Charles Fay is a parent, business owner, internationally acclaimed consultant, and author of numerous books, articles, audios, and videos. Educators, mental health professionals, and parents around the world have profited from his practical, down-to-earth solutions to the most challenging problems displayed by youth of all ages. These solutions come from years of research and experience serving severely disturbed youth in psychiatric hospital, public school, and home settings.

Dr. Fay was also a bratty little brother to two older sisters. Through this early life research on how to annoy them, he developed a clear understanding of the mental makeup of sibling warriors—as well as how to help parents tame them.

INTRODUCTION

First the bad news. Since the very dawn of civilization, brothers and sisters have bickered and argued with one another, and parents have been caught in the crossfire. Where there are siblings, there will be rivalry. You can't make them love each other, you can't make them get along, and there is no silver bullet that will tame the savage beast and transform them into civil human beings who will make your home a utopia of brotherly and sisterly love. If there were, there would be no need for parents. We could just wave that magic wand, tap them on the heads, and send them out to face the world neither fearing for their safety from the world nor for the safety of the world from them!

But here is the good news: Sibling battles need not destroy your sanity. You don't have to get caught in the crossfire. In this book you will learn some basic techniques for how to step out of the line of fire—and when you do, your kids will start solving problems for themselves. They will start developing coping and conflict resolution skills that will last a lifetime! There will be more moments of peace and harmony in your home, because your kids are learning how to end their own disputes before you ever have to get involved.

Certainly it is a process—as are all aspects of raising kids—but if you will apply the two simple rules of Love and Logic, it won't take you long to start seeing improvement. Your life will get better right away and so will theirs. Over time they will begin acting like those civil human beings we are all hoping for. Love and Logic isn't magic, but it does significantly up the odds that your kids will become highly competent, responsible, and proud adults.

In this book, we'll discuss the two rules of Love and Logic, and how they apply to dealing with sibling spats. They are pretty simple, so I want to give them to you now.

THE RULES OF LOVE AND LOGIC

RULE ONE
Adults set firm limits in loving ways without anger, lecture, threats, or repeated warnings.

- Adults set limits they are able to enforce.
- Adults take care of themselves in loving ways.
- Adults make their home resemble the real world as much as possible.

RULE TWO
When children misbehave and cause problems, adults hand these problems back in loving ways.

- Adults understand that lessons learned from small mistakes early in life are far more affordable than large mistakes made later in life.
- Adults remember to provide strong doses of empathy before providing consequences.
- Children are given the gift of owning and solving their problems.

Love and Logic parents understand that the "price tag" of mistakes goes up every day. As a result, they see problems as opportunities for kids to learn when consequences are still small. Every conflict is a chance for our children to develop skills to handle situations in their own healthy way. It is an opening for them to build confidence in their ability to resolve disputes—and learn that you believe them completely competent to do so. Love and Logic turns parents from adversaries into advisors as they stand with their kids to help resolve issues rather than as judge and jury handing out verdicts and sentences.

One of the goals of Love and Logic is to leave our kids more tired at the end of the day than we are, because they have been working harder than we have on keeping the peace with their siblings. Good things happen when kids have to think really hard about their problems and come up with solutions. When they go out into the world and we're not with them, they'll be equipped to do just fine, because they developed these problem-solving skills when they were youngsters.

Before we get into the specifics of applying Love and Logic principles to sibling disputes and disagreements, we need to better understand the philosophies and practices behind Love and Logic. With that in mind, the first three chapters of this book give you the basics of Love and Logic, as well as some brief examples of how to apply these basics to sibling spats. Those of you new to Love and Logic will learn the foundational skills essential for making parenting fun rather than frantic. Those familiar with our approach will get the repetition we all need to learn and remember these foundational skills. These include:

- How to set limits without waging war.
- How to put an end to arguing and manipulation.
- How to stay calm when your kids aren't.
- How to provide consequences in a way that will help your kids learn responsibility rather than resentment.

In the final two chapters, I'll give you an even more specific step-by-step plan for staying cool in the midst of heated sibling battles and for helping your kids learn to take responsibility for resolving their own issues. These are neither theory nor complicated psycho-babble-laden techniques, but practical, down-to-earth, anyone-can-apply-it tools for parents who want long-term solutions to sibling rivalry. I have also dug into the Love and Logic archives to give you real-life examples of how it has worked for others. This is rubber-meets-the-pavement stuff. It is the stuff I was raised with and that I am raising my kids with—I have a twenty-three-year-old stepson, a fourteen-year-old son, and I have a one-year old son (yeah, I'm kind of surprised about that last one, too). When I remember to practice what I preach, it really works. It will also help you raise respectful, responsible, and hearty kids who've got what it takes to survive and excel in today's challenging world.

Dr. Charles Fay

CHAPTER ONE

The Price Tag Goes Up Every Day

Despite centuries of human invention and progress, our world today is much more complicated than it was just a century ago, and with that have come new dangers and pitfalls for our children. Our more sophisticated society demands more sophisticated kids to navigate it, and in turn demands more out of us as parents. If our kids are going to survive in today's complex, dangerous world, they're going to need to know how to make good choices in the midst of a multitude of voices influencing them to make bad ones. They will need a lot of practice encountering struggles, making decisions about how to handle those struggles, and then learning from the consequences of their decisions. In other words, our kids will need to make plenty of mistakes when they are younger—when the stakes are low—so that they don't have to make them as adults—when the costs of their mistakes may be life and death.

Kids don't just jump out of bed one day and find themselves able to handle anything life might throw at them. They have to be trained, and their training is our job as parents. Here's the problem: Have you ever noticed what happens when we try to lecture a strong-willed child? Have you ever noticed how many of our wise words seem to go in one ear then right out the other? Why is this the case? Simply because strong-willed kids learn best by making mistakes and experiencing the consequences *for themselves.*

For kids, the road to wisdom is paved with little life lessons. This is a scary responsibility for us as parents, but there is truly no more important—or potentially rewarding—responsibility on earth.

Because of this, Love and Logic parents actually hope and pray, each and every day, that their kids will encounter learning opportunities as early and often in their lives as possible. They hope and pray that their kids have to make a lot of decisions about how to handle life, and that they fail regularly when the stakes are low. They hope that their kids learn from those failures so that when mistakes cost much more, they are able to make better decisions. You see, every single day of our kids' lives, the price tag of their mistakes goes up. Let me say this again:

Love and Logic parents hope and pray their kids make lots and lots of little mistakes as they're coping with life's small challenges. Why? So that they have a strong understanding of cause and effect when they are older and their mistakes may have life and death consequences.

The road to wisdom is paved with little mistakes...
and their consequences.

When Siblings Clash

When Patrice was born, she took one look at her older brother, Brett, and summed up in an instant he needed some improvements. It was literally a sibling battle from the get go. Whenever she discovered something she felt was sub-par in her brother, she let him know, and if he didn't do something about it pretty quick, she went to a higher authority. So, by the time she was seven and Brett was ten, if they weren't bickering, she was tattling that "Brett's picking his buggers!" or "Brett won't clean up his mess!" Brett wasn't one who appreciated having a second mom, either, as he was having trouble enough keeping up with the first one, so he found ways to retaliate when he could. No lectures or good talking to's had any effect either. If they were near each other, they were bickering or squabbling. The constant conflict was driving their parents up the wall. What were they to do?

Little Lawrence and his twin brother Robert might have looked alike, but it seemed they were different in every other way. Though only toddlers, they spat like cats and dogs, and were constantly at each other. Because of their age, the twins' mom and dad weren't sure what to do, as all of the techniques for handling sibling fights they had heard seemed too sophisticated for their youngsters. Mom and Dad could find no reasonable way of ending the fighting until they came to me directly for help. How do you think they solved the problem?

Tucker and Hunter were teenage boys in the same home, though they couldn't have been more naturally different had they been born on opposite sides of the planet. Tucker was artistic and random; Hunter logical and scientific. Hunter was quiet and liked to be on his own; Tucker was social and had a tendency to be loud and enthusiastic. They came out of the womb antagonistic opposites and never failed to get into battles when they were together. So, as a rule, they went their separate ways—but that failed to work when they had to go somewhere in the car. For a long time they fought over who got "shotgun" until the battle got so crazy Mom had to make them both sit in the back all of the time. Now, of course, it would never be long before they started bickering and battling anew. Mom came up with a creative way of applying Love and Logic to the situation that I thought was brilliant. What do you think she did?

Can you identify with any of these situations? Most of us can. Yet all of these were solved with the simple steps we are going to explore in the following chapters. Keep them in mind as you read and come up with your own creative solutions. In the last chapter, I will let you in on what these parents did to end the mayhem caused by these siblings in their homes and you can match their solutions up with your own.

As parents, we have to turn our thinking around a bit to see the advantages in sibling rivalry rather than the problems. The blessing of sibling rivalry is the many significant learning opportunities it provides! So when it rears its ugly head, what should we be saying to ourselves? "Thank goodness! Another opportunity for my kids to ı̴̶ａ̶ı̶n cause and effect and how to solve problems for themselves." That's right, because every little conflict provides a precious opportunity for our kids to make some little mistakes, and through those mistakes to develop problem-solving and coping skills that will benefit them later in life.

Every little sibling spat provides a wonderful opportunity for our kids to develop problem-solving and coping skills.

Believe it or not, Love and Logic was really inspired by sibling rivalry—more specifically, my back seat battles with my sisters.

The Historic Battle of the Station Wagon

My parents started learning this stuff about the time I was in kindergarten. They didn't have Love and Logic growing up so they had to learn it when I was growing up. I remember going on a vacation—I must have been about five years old—and we all piled into Dad's 1969 Chrysler Town and Country station wagon. You know, the kind with the fake wood paneling on the side? I was sitting in the backseat in the middle of my two sisters, Suzie on one side and Nancy on the other, and guess what? There were little seams of vinyl piping that ran down the seat on each of my sides. Now, are those merely decorations in the seat? No, every kid knows that those are actually the boundaries between sovereign nations. If you go over that line, you have invaded someone else's territory. It's the equivalent of violating a treaty or declaring war. We were heading north on I-25 out of Colorado, and then we start heading east on I-80 through the lower part of Wyoming—now that's some exciting country, let me tell you.

Well, it didn't take long before I started getting bored, so I looked at one of my sisters. You know how that works, right? The next thing you know, she whines, "Dad, Dad, Charlie is looking at me!"

When my father was younger, he really only had one parenting skill, and it sounded like this, "Well, for crying out loud!" He never whispered this skill because he believed at that time the louder you yelled the more effective you were. My mother also only had one skill, and she learned this skill from her mother who learned it from her mother, who learned it from all the other mothers going way back to the Carpathians Mountains of Eastern Europe. It sounded like this, "You keep behaving that way, gypsies come." So there were my two parents, each with one skill apiece.

At this particular juncture, my father decided not to use his one skill at all, so he just stared out the windshield. My mother, on the other hand, pretended to sleep. Well, that wasn't any fun, so I decided to up the ante; I reached over and actually touched one of my sisters. She, of course, said, "Dad, he's touching me! Make him stop!" But my father just stared straight ahead out the windshield and my mother pretended to sleep.

It wasn't long before I had to really raise the ante. I had to go for the ultimate irritation. The next thing you knew, both of my sisters were yelling, "Dad, Dad! Charlie's making smells. Make him stop."

Right then and there Dad snapped. He turned around all the way in the seat, and he started waving his hand around trying to grab someone. He would have been happy to get any of us, I think. Meanwhile my sisters and I had our little heads and bodies pressed firmly against the back of the seat. We could feel the wind from his waving hand, so we settled down right away. Why? Was it because that was an effective skill? No. It was because we could see the eighteen-wheeler coming the other way and he couldn't. Luckily he recovered in time to miss it.

Well, eventually we ended up at our vacation destination of Minden, Nebraska, home of Pioneer Village. (By the way, if you're unfamiliar with Pioneer Village, it's one of the world's neatest living history museums—but not to me as a five-year-old.) I remember thinking to myself, "They're making soap? This place stinks. I thought this was going to be fun. They told us how great it would be. Randy's parents took him to Disneyland and we get to sit around and watch a bunch of psychotic people making soap. Don't they know they can buy soap?" Then I let it slip. "This is boring."

My dad looked at me and yelled, " You don't know the kind of sacrifices we've had to make to take you on this trip. You think we enjoyed driving all the way out here?" In response I started to cry.

A little tear started to drip down my face, and he said, "Don't you cry or I'll give you something to cry about." It was really a great trip for everyone.

So, all the way back to Denver, my parents no longer had kids, they had little monsters in the backseat, kicking the seat, squabbling with each other, and stepping on the seatbelt. Do you remember those old cars that had the seatbelts mounted on the floor? If you got upset with your parents all you had to do was step on the seatbelt a little bit and it would tighten around them in the front. It was utter chaos. We had to stop at every single, dirty, filling-station restroom on I-80 and I-25 all the way home.

The trip turned out to be an inspiration. My parents grew so desperate because of that trip that they started studying how to be better parents, and it didn't take them long to learn a few things.

But the trip turned out to be an inspiration. My parents grew so desperate because of that trip that they started studying how to be better parents, and it didn't take them long to learn a few things.

No More Hassles

I remember we were in Penney's Department Store not long after that in the shoe department. I got bored again—and when things got boring, I knew hassling a sister or two was always a great way to spice things up. So I started bugging them. I remember my mother leaned over and I thought, "Here comes the gypsy bit." But she didn't say it. All she said was, "Ooh, Charlie, that looks like a really bad decision."

I was confused. I didn't know what to make of that, but eventually we got in the car and went home.

All my mom said was, "Ooh, Charlie, that looks like a really bad decision."

Then a couple days later, my parents were getting ready to go out. I asked, "Mom, where are we going?"

She said, "Well, we're going to go and watch a movie over at Cinderella City."

I said, "Oh, yeah! I like the movies over there."

Then she looked at me sadly and said, "Oh, but the sad part is you're not coming."

"But I want to come!" I cried back. "And I'm just a little kid, I can't stay here all by myself."

Right then the doorbell rang. When I answered it, the earth shook as she entered. There was no space between the doorframe and her awesome body. Yes, it was Mabel, the babysitter from hell. I took one look at her and whimpered, "I don't want to stay with her. She looks like she's mean."

My father came to my aid, "Hmmm, she could be, but hang in there. Make friends with her." Then he added, "By the way, how are you going to pay her?"

I was shocked. "I don't have any money," I whimpered.

My dad answered, "Well, probably best not to worry about it then."

And of course what did I do? I worried.

Now Mabel wasn't that bad. In fact she took really good care of me—but she was really, really boring.

It wasn't long before we ended up in another boring situation in another boring department store, and I thought to myself, "You know what? It's boring, and I know what to do when it's boring. Hassle a sister or two." So I started to hassle my sisters, and my mother looked at me, then she leaned over and started to say, "Ooh… " but I snapped to attention so fast she didn't get a chance to finish. I remember it being that very day that my little head began thinking, "I don't want this to be a bad decision."

I remember it being that very day that my little head began thinking, "I don't want this to be a bad decision."

The Three E's

And that is exactly how we want our kids to start thinking if we are Love and Logic parents. While we can't make our kids love each

can control whether or not we provide the three Es of Logic. What are those three Es?

The first E stands for example. A huge key to Love and Logic is all about what you do yourself that no one else has control over. While you can't control your kids' loving each other or stop them from starting fights, you can control your reactions to them when they are battling and model for them correct responses to such challenges. This is the double-edged sword of Love and Logic, and both edges work in your favor. The first is they see an adult handle problems without losing their cool, lecturing, threatening, or rashly trying to bluff their way into getting others to cooperate with them. The second is that when we think in terms of what we can do and not try to control what our kids are doing, we can never lose control of a situation.

You know what I hope? I hope your kids see you having conflicts with other adults. I hope your kids see you having conflicts with your spouse, and what I pray for is that your kids see you and your spouse working through your disagreements in a healthy way. Because if they don't, they will not have reference points for solving marital spats when they are older—or their spats with each other. My parents both came from families where there was a good amount of yelling and unhealthy communication (you may have guessed that from the parenting techniques they started with), so early in their marriage they decided they would never let us kids see them disagree with each other. As a result, it was about forty years before I realized that conflict is an essential and healthy part of life. I had no roadmap for how to handle that, so I had to work it out for myself. One of the best things we can do for our kids is have plenty of little conflicts in front of them, and let them see how people come to compromises and concessions and solve disagreements in a mature way.

....

The three E's of Love and Logic are
1) **example**, 2) **experience**, *and* 3) **empathy**.

....

The second E of Love and Logic is experience. It's the lucky kid that has parents who are brave enough to let him or her make plenty of little mistakes. And even luckier kids have parents who are also loving enough to hold them firmly accountable for their poor decisions by letting them face the consequences of those decisions and learn from them.

Now please don't misunderstand this. Love and Logic is not about abandoning our kids to the fate of their decisions. While kids face consequences, we stand right there and go through the fire with them. Ultimately one of the great bonuses of Love and Logic is improving our relationships with our children, not distancing ourselves from them. When we take the anger, lectures, threats, and repeated warnings out of our parent-child communications, there is a lot more room for other kinds of communications that are a ton more fun and bring us closer together. What we experience together with our kids builds bonds that are strengthened all the more because our kids know we are confident in their ability to handle and overcome the outcomes of their decisions. Kids thrive when they know their parents believe in them.

The third E of Love and Logic is, of course, empathy. When all of this is delivered with sincere understanding instead of anger, what happens? It locks the lesson in so that kids develop a voice inside of their heads—like the one I had—that says, "When I make bad decisions, it doesn't necessarily make other people mad, but it may really affect the quality of my own life. So before I make this next decision, I am going to think really, really hard about it and try to make it a good one."

Are You *Really* Serious?

Now I know how crazy all this might sound as it flies in the face of what many people think parenting is all about: protecting our kids from life's discomforts and trying to provide them with a more contented childhood than we ourselves had. However, as I was learning about parenting when I became a parent myself, I had the good fortune to live right next door to one of those wonderfully wise, commonsense parents who think childhood is about training kids to be able to handle the world rather than being protected from it. Her name was Jane.

By the time I met Jane she was about eighty years old, and she'd raised a whole slew of really great people. It wasn't long after we got to know each other that we started talking about Love and Logic. I even gave her one of the books. She took it home, and not a week later she came running across the yard waving it. She said, "Our Pa used this before you guys ever came up with it."

I said, "Really, Jane?"

And she said, "Yes. Anytime my Pa saw us squabbling and fussing with each other, he'd just say this, 'Oh, it breaks my heart to see my young 'uns fussing and squabbling like that. Y'all must have too much time on your hands, but I think I can help with that. Now, I bet if you went over there with your brother and you pulled them weeds outside the barn that would give you lots of practice figuring out how to get along rather than fight all of the time.' Every single time we squabbled with each other and fussed around him, he'd come up with some chore for us to do, so we could practice getting along."

I had to wonder at this, so I asked, "Jane, did that really help?"

She said, "Well, it didn't always make us love each other, but we got real good at pretending like we did." Then she added, "The strangest thing was that the more we pretended like we loved each other, the more we did actually love each other."

"The strangest thing was that the more we pretended like we loved each other, the more we did actually love each other."

Your Kids Will Be Happier When You Are Happier

I learned a lot from Jane. One of the things I learned is that successful parents waste lots of energy trying to nag and lecture their kids into loving each other. They don't preoccupy themselves with trying to figure out who started what argument, and they don't burn up a bunch of effort trying to get their kids to apologize to each other. If you are like me, you have tried that before. I can't count how many times I have heard, "*Sorry*," and known it was neither meant nor received with any real impact on my kids' relationship.

However, all of the wonderfully wise parents I've met over the years handle such disputes differently. They know it doesn't matter what they lecture their kids about, because their kids' eyes will just glaze over when they say more than two sentences together. What matters the most is how they handle the bickering. These wise parents let consequences—logical, meaningful, natural consequences—teach their kids that there are better ways to solve differences of opinion than fighting.

But there's something even more important about these wise parents. They never forget who the conflict really belongs to in the first place. They don't steal precious learning opportunities from their kids. Whose problem are those sibling battles, after all? That's right. They belong to your kids—so why should you deny them these precious learning opportunities?

The truly successful parents we've met don't:
- Burn up lots of energy trying to nag and lecture their kids into loving each other.
- Preoccupy themselves with trying to figure out who started what argument.
- Burn up a bunch of effort trying to get their kids to apologize to each other.

These great parents do:
- Let logical consequences do the teaching.
- Remember that the sibling rivalry problem is not theirs to solve—it's their kid's.
- Take good care of themselves so that they can be loving.

Now, it is true that our kids' fighting can become our problem because the noise hassles our ears and tears at our hearts because we want our kids to love each other. But wise parents realize that even in helping to solve problems, the initial cause of their trouble still remains in the kids' court. Because what happens when we own and solve our kids' problems for them rather than giving them an opportunity to solve problems for themselves? Two things happen—neither of which are good. We get worn out and they learn nothing. Then we start having fantasies about how wonderful it would be if we didn't have kids anymore. Isn't that sad? Because kids really are a blessing after all, aren't they? They're little miracles walking around the earth, but when we become exhausted from handling all of their problems, it is easy to forget that. So Love and Logic parents take good care of themselves so that they never forget how wonderful their kids really are.

> *Love and Logic parents take good care of themselves so that they never forget how wonderful their kids really are.*

Have you noticed that this book gives you permission to take good care of yourself? Isn't it refreshing to hear that great parents do that? Why is this so important? Well, one of the main reasons is that if we model taking care of ourselves, we teach our kids to take care of themselves. We teach them not to get dragged into other people's problems or allow others to intimidate and manipulate them into doing what they want rather than what our kids know is right. That is a pretty valuable lesson, don't you agree? Another reason is that taking care of ourselves makes sure we have the energy—both mentally and physically—to be the fun, loving parent we want to be. Love and Logic parents aren't burnt out, so when their kids are ready to be fun, so are they!

Are you ready for more tips for staying sane? Read on!

CHAPTER TWO

Rule One

Now, let's take some time to look at the two rules of Love and Logic more specifically. Again, here is the first one:

> **RULE ONE**
> **Adults set limits without anger, lectures, threats, or repeated warnings.**

Now I know you may be thinking that this kind of takes the fun out of it. I mean, where's the joy in disciplining our kids if we can't rant and rave at them? Well, that might have worked when our kids are very young, but when they are able to rant and rave back, parenting that way can turn sour pretty quickly. Love and Logic rules are there to keep that from happening. They are also there to give our kids the kind of loving leadership they need.

The Importance of Enforceable Limits

Humans yearn for leadership in the form of loving, yet firm limits. In families where there are no solid boundaries, there will always be a problem with kids getting along with each other. In a company where there is no solid leadership, there will always be a problem with employees getting along with each other. In schools where there is no strong leadership, there will be problems with the teachers and staff not getting along with each other. And in classrooms where there aren't solid limits, there will be problems with the students not getting along with each other. Why? Because human beings crave leadership and the security of clear, understandable, enforceable limits. When these limits are absent, a leadership vacuum develops. It doesn't take long for the kids to start battling for the position of top dog. When effective limits are present, kids don't feel such a need. So how do we give such limits to our kids?

Okay, time for a test.

I'm going to set some limits right now, and if you think the limit is clear and enforceable, pick "Gold"; if it isn't, and it is just going to lead into a fight, label it "Garbage." Cover up the footnotes, and then check them after you have answered each of these to see how many you got right.

1. "Quit yelling for crying out loud." Gold or garbage?
2. "I only listen to calm quiet voices." Gold or garbage?
3. "Quit interrupting each other. How I am supposed to figure out what's wrong if everybody talks at the same time?" Gold or garbage?
4. "I listen to one person at a time."
5. "Cut it out back there. You don't want me to stop this car."
6. What if I add, "I'm serious!"
7. "I drive when it's quiet and it's safe."
8. "I charge $2.00 a minute to listen to that kind of stuff. Keep it up."
9. "As soon as I get off this phone, both of you are going to get it. I mean it!"
10. "How come you guys never get along over that? See there's a lot of kids that don't even have a Nintendo. Don't you understand that that's a privilege? What? I didn't hear what you said. Do you understand? You need to share."
11. "Hey, guess what? You guys get to have that as long as I don't hear any bickering whatsoever."

1. Garbage, 2. Gold, 3. Garbage, 4. Gold, 5. Garbage, 6. Still garbage, 7. Gold, 8. Gold, 9. Garbage, 10. Garbage, 11. Gold.

It's not rocket science to tell the difference, is it? My guess is you got every one of these correct. What's the common thread? *You can't set effective limits by telling other people what to do, only what you are going to do.* Love and Logic parents set effective limits by describing what they're going to do and what they're going to allow.

> *You can't set effective limits by telling other people what to do, only what you are going to do.*

There's a big difference between saying something like this, "You better treat me with respect," and "Hey, guess what? I'll be happy to do the extra things I do for you when I feel respected." There's also a big difference between saying, "You know, I am sick and tired of having to—" and "I drive kids places they want to go when I'm all charged up. And right now I'm all drained out. You know why I'm so drained? Because I've been listening to stuff like, 'He flicked a booger on me,' or 'He's looking at me.'" And that is what? Gold or Garbage?

Gold. That's right. Enforceable limits are always gold.

Making Limits Practical

Another aspect of enforceable statements is they are something we, as the parent, can do without help from or dependence upon anyone else. Powerful people don't boss other people around; they set limits by describing what they will put up with and what they will do. They take care of themselves so that they can give others the security of loving leadership. Let me give you some more examples of unenforceable versus enforceable statements so that it is easier to see the difference:

Unenforceable Statement (i.e. "Garbage")	Enforceable Statement (i.e. "Gold")
Quit fighting over that!	I'll drive when it's quiet and safe.
Stop it back there!	You may stay in this room with me as long as I don't have to hear your arguing.
Why can't you just get along?	You may play with that as long as there is no fighting.
Quit interrupting each other!	I listen to one person at a time.
Who started it?	I charge one dollar per minute for listening to sibling hassles.
You guys are driving me nuts!	Kids who don't get along around here get to do extra chores.
Can't we just have a peaceful dinner?	Kid who make dinner unpleasant get to eat theirs in the garage.

There's an even simpler way to get started using enforceable statements. Just use the following generic formula:

Step one: Start by saying either:
"Feel free to . . ."
"You may . . ."
"I allow. . . ."

Step two: Continue by filling in what you'll be setting the limit over. For example:
"I allow kids *to play with that . . .*"
"Feel free *to join us at the table . . .*"
"You may *have your friend over . . .*"

16

Step three: End the statement with

" . . . *as long as it does not cause a problem.*"

So the entire thing might sound something like this:

"Feel free to watch television with your brother, *as long as it doesn't cause a problem.*"

Step four: Some people like to tack an additional caveat onto this that goes

" . . . *for anyone in the universe.*"

So now the statement goes something like:

"Feel free to watch TV with your brother as long as it does not cause a problem *for anyone in the universe.*"

Gold or garbage? That's right, gold.

Now, what happens if watching TV does cause a problem (which, more often than not, it seems to)? Then it is pretty simple to turn the TV off—or, if needed, once the kids are out of the house, unplug the set and put it in storage. The limit is simple, straightforward, and *easily enforceable.*

Let me give you another example: "You may have your friend Travis over *as long as there are no problems for anyone in the universe.*" Again, direct and simple. And if there is a problem with Travis, guess what? Travis goes home. He can come back another day, but for the rest of that day he is gone, and before he comes back there will be some thought given to how to make sure there are no problems for anyone in the universe the next time he visits.

Or how about this one, "I'll be happy to take you to the amusement park as long as there are no problems."

You can plug anything in there and it will work. Why? Because it has to do with *what you will allow* and *what you can do.* You are not giving commands you can't make happen. You are not telling your kids to behave, because truthfully, you may have no control over that, but you are telling them that if they misbehave, privileges will be taken away, because you can turn the TV off or take Travis home.

You can plug anything in this formula and it will work.
Why? Because it has to do with what you will allow
and what you can do.

Now I want to tell you a little secret. Please don't share it with anybody else. Do we have a solemn oath? Okay. Here it is:

Love and Logic has nothing to do with setting limits on kids;
what Love and Logic is all about is setting limits on parents.

That's right. By setting limits on ourselves and what we will allow, we parents get the upper hand because there is no more bluffing and trying to manipulate our kids. All we need is this simple approach for coming up with statements that are actually enforceable and that we can back up—then the resolve to lovingly and consistently enforce them whenever we need to.

Give It Your Own Twist

A lady in Detroit, Michigan, modified this generic enforceable statement just a bit in order to solve a sibling dispute in her home. Apparently her boys were constantly battling over the television remote control. It was a terrible ongoing struggle, and one day when they were fighting over it, she walked up to them and she said, "Guys?"

They said, "What, Mom? You're making us miss our show."

She said, "Hey, I'll be happy to allow TV as long as it causes no brain damage."

Apparently they thought that was pretty stupid. They said, "Mom, that's like some kind of urban legend or something. TV doesn't cause brain damage."

She responded, "You know, you're right. TV doesn't cause brain damage. The brain damage I'm talking about is the brain damage I get from listening to you guys fighting over the remote. So, feel free to have TV as long as I don't have any brain damage over it."

And you know what? Like all strong-willed kids worth keeping, they ignored her. They watched their TV and they argued and they refused to shut it off when she asked, but she didn't sa' beyond the limit she had given earlier.

The very next day, when they got home from school, right where the TV used to be was a nice little table. And on that table was a wonderful little portrait of their family. The boys said, "Mom, where's the TV?"

And she said, "Ohhhhh, I have to tell you. It's terrible. I got brain damage."

"Oh, you're crazy!"

Then she just answered, "I know," and wouldn't say anything else besides "I know" for the rest of the conversation. The boys were initially irate, but they got over it rather quickly.

However, that is not the end of the story. In fact, this mom got really freaked out by what happened next. She told me, "You know, about three days later, my house seemed really eerie—it was so quiet. Then as I looked out the window while I was washing dishes, I saw two of my boys out there, and guess what they were doing? Playing. I have to admit that kind of shocked me because they never had played together outside before without me throwing them out of the house. Then I heard a noise in my daughter's room and I rushed in there and it sent shivers up my spine! She had this strange thing in her hand. It was a book."

Is it okay if I go on a little caveat right now? Can I stand on a soapbox for a moment? I truly wish more parents understood the following:

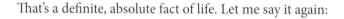

The more TV kids watch, the more problems they're going to have.

That's a definite, absolute fact of life. Let me say it again:

The more TV your kids watch, the more problems they will have with attention, the more problems they will have in school, the more problems they will have with self-control, and the more problems they will have with each other.

Take a night and just soak in how people relate to each other on many television shows. Then ask yourself, "Do I really want my kids to be copying this?" Because, when we let them watch too much television that is exactly what they will do, and the same dysfunction TV families have will be exemplified in your home every night.

While limiting TV can go a long way to solving this, there are some kids that should not have TV at all. There are some families who shouldn't even have a television in the house. In families that are healthy and where everybody gets along, it's fine to have some TV. If your kids are at each other's throats more often than not, TV is really the last thing that they ought to be spending their time on.

If your kids are at each other's throats more often than not, TV is really the last thing that they ought to be spending their time on.

If you want a more peaceful home, give this some thought.

Ending the Power Struggle

Human beings—that means your kids, too—yearn for loving leadership in the form of enforceable limits. As I mentioned earlier, when limits are absent, what happens? A leadership vacuum develops and pretty quickly your kids will start fighting with each other to fill the position.

One of the ways that kids test the strength of loving leadership is by arguing with their parents to see if their parents will lose control of themselves by either getting angry or backing down. Either response is a victory for kids, but you should never lose an argument with your kids on account of either. We parents lose disputes with our kids because we let ourselves get drawn into emotional altercations with them over the limits we've set. We get trapped by thinking we have to convince our kids that we are right rather than simply holding to what's right and letting logical consequences do the teaching.

We need to be confident our limits are just whether our kids agree or not, and then hold to them. Even more importantly, we need to be willing to pay the price to enforce limits when our kids are young—and the consequences are relatively low—so that they learn self-control and how to make better decisions before the consequences are very costly.

How do we let the limits and the consequences do the teaching without getting dragged into fighting about them? How do we avoid giving up our authority by getting pulled into un-winnable arguments?

Of course, we know that some kids will fight until their breath is gone to draw us into a struggle. How do we stay calm when they push our emotional buttons? Many parents find it helpful to think ahead and consider the types of "hooks" their kids use to pull them into arguments. Listed below are some classics:

You never loved me.
Not fair! He always gets to—
You love him/her more than me!
All the other kids get to—
None of the other kids have to—
Not fair! He/She started it!
Why do you always take his/her side?
You're not our real mom!

Do your kids use any of these to push your buttons? If they are normal they do! They've probably come up with a few creative ones that aren't on this list! Here's the problem: When our buttons get pushed it's pretty darn hard to remember any of our parenting skills. It's tough to stick to the limits we set. It's hard to avoid lecturing or even threatening. It's even difficult for some parents to resist the urge to strike out at their kids verbally—or physically. There's one sure thing about allowing our kids to push our buttons: They come to believe that they can get what they want by being manipulative.

> *We need to be confident our limits are just whether our kids agree or not, and then hold to them.*

Besides thinking ahead about the typical "hooks" they use, how do we know when a kid is starting to push our buttons? For me it's a feeling that starts at my feet, climbs to my stomach, then runs up into my chest, and results in me thinking, "I know how to handle

tion, but right now I'm not going to use those skills. I'm going to get it on with this kid. Yes, I'm going to have a major power struggle that I can't win, but I'll mop up the damage later." Have you ever been there? I certainly have.

Go Brain Dead: Do Not Think

So what do we do when we start having that feeling? Go brain dead. We can't allow ourselves to think about what our kids are saying. Why? Because if we think too hard about what our kids are saying, what will happen? Well, if you're like me, silly lectures will uncontrollably spew right out of your mouth.

For example, have you ever heard an interaction like this? "You know one of these days you better learn your lesson because you are going to value a relationship with your sister. Now, you better say you're sorry. I mean it! Listen. You're lucky to have—I mean, there are a lot of kids who don't have siblings, and then they grow up and wish they had had that kind of close relationship. I mean it!" Do you know any kids in their right mind who would respond, "Well, that makes a lot of sense. We really ought to start bonding a little bit." Of course not.

Reasoning with angry, arguing kids is about as effective as fighting a forest fire with gasoline. Don't try to match wits with an angry, arguing kid. They will out-stupid you every time!

Reasoning with angry, arguing kids is about as effective as fighting a forest fire with gasoline.

So it's helpful to master the art of going brain dead in the midst of arguments with your kids, and it goes something like this: *In a very loving way, after you have set your limit, repeat the same phrase over and over again like a broken record.*

Listed below are some favorite Love and Logic "one-liners":

I love you too much to argue.
I know.
Thanks for letting me know how you feel.

I bet it feels that way.
Ohhhh.
I'll listen when your voice is calm.
Probably so.
What did I say?

One of my very favorites is that first one: "Love you too much to argue." Here's a sample dialogue between a Love and Logic parent and one of their kids:

Child: "Well, you never loved me."
Parent (calmly): "Love you too much to argue."
Child: "Don't use that Love and Logic crap on me."
Parent: "Love you too much to argue."
Child: "But that doesn't even make sense."
Parent: "Love you too much to argue."
Child: "Well, I'm just going to leave."
Parent: "Love you too much to argue."

Notice that Love and Logic parents don't get too creative! They just stick with the very same one-liner. Following this strategy, they quickly find their kids arguing less and behaving sweeter.

Ohhhhhhhh

A lot of parents fail at this because they can't come up with that one-liner in the heat of battle, and the truth of the matter is you shouldn't. You have to have your one-liner ready and loaded long before your next altercation. So here is another all-time favorite—just say, "Ohhhhh," and draw it out like a squeaking door being opened very slowly. Make sure that you let all the air out of your lungs when you say it. Why? First of all, it's relaxing, and secondly, when the air is all out of your lungs, you can't say anything more. So here we go again:

Child: "Yeah, but you let him—"
Parent: "Ohhhhhhh."

: "What are you smoking?"

Parent: "Ohhhhhhh."

Child: "You're freaking me out."

Parent: "Ohhhhhhh."

Child: "I'm calling social services."

Parent: "Ohhhhhhh."

Child: "Well, this is stupid!" Then they roll their eyes and
walk away.

Great work!

Now, another thing that's helpful is if you nod like you're taking
it all in while they are ranting. "Wow." "Yeah." "Yeah." "Uh-huh."
"Yeah." That's one of the skills I learned as a psychologist—just keep
listening and give them cues to keep talking. Typically what happens is they'll burn up all of their energy talking—and you'll save
all of your energy being completely brain dead. Remember one of
the major goals of Love and Logic:

> *Kids should always be more tired at the end of the day*
> *than their parents are.*

Of course, you should find something that suits you. Some
people like, "I know," like the lady in Detroit. My dad used to like,
"What a bummer." Just find something that fits you and then repeat
it over and over and over again until they get the message that it is
the only thing you are going to say for the rest of the conversation.
Discussion over. You, the parent, will do no more to address this
problem, and you are not going to argue about it.

Now—and we will discuss this in more detail in the next chapter—your one-liner needs to be said with genuine empathy for your
kids, and without a hint of either sarcasm or anger. If we express
no empathy in our one-liners, the issue again becomes us inflicting
things on our kids—trying to get even with them for the stress and
anxiety they are putting us through—and not the problem itself.

Anger and sarcasm are forms of losing the argument by losing
control of ourselves, and the focus becomes us versus our kids.

24

However, if we let genuine concern for our kids show through our one-liners, we let our kids know it is us *and* them against the problem. We are on their side, and glad to help by giving advice and ideas, but we are also completely confident that they can solve the problem on their own. By doing this, we leave the problem in their court and let them go off to do the bulk of the thinking about how to resolve it.

More Wisdom from My Neighbor Jane

When I discussed this with my neighbor Jane, she responded, "I used to argue with my Pa."

I said, "No, you didn't."

"Yeah, I did. I'm telling you."

Perplexed, I asked, "What'd you say to him?"

"Well," she said, "sometimes me and my brother, we'd start arguing with him, and we'd say stuff like this, 'Well, Pa, we really don't want to do that.'" (Now, that was major defiance on the farm seventy years ago. Have times changed a little bit?)

I had to know. "Well, what would he do, Jane?"

"Well, he just smiled." (Why do you smile at an arguing kid? It kind of confuses them, doesn't it? There's another basic rule of parenting. The more confused they are, the easier they are to deal with.)

"Then what did your Pa say?" I asked.

"Well, he would just smile and say this, 'Well, Sweet Jane, no time for making kitten britches.'"

Now I was really confused. "Jane, that's weird."

"I know," she said, "but he'd just keep saying that. 'No time for making kitten britches.' It got to the point that he didn't even have to say the whole thing. See, we'd start talking back a little bit, and he'd say, 'Well . . . ' and we'd say 'No time for making kitten britches' and know we were beaten."

"Jane, that is really a strange saying. What does it mean?"

She paused, then said, "You know, I still don't know, but I tell you what, when I started to have my own kids and they started to argue with me, it just came out of my mouth. And I thought, 'It ain't fair to be using something on a kid when you don't know what it means,' so I called up my Pa and asked, 'Pa, you remember when you used to say 'no time for making kitten britches'? And Pa said, 'Yep.' 'Well, what's it mean?' And he said, 'I don't know.' So I asked him, 'Well, why did you say it then?' And Pa said, 'Well, Sweet Jane, I just got to figuring that when a kid says something that ain't too bright, you ought to match it up.'"

"I just got to figuring that when a kid says something that ain't too bright, you ought to match it up."

I realized right then and there that that was one of the most brilliant things I had ever heard. Think for a minute about how wise that is. When a kid says something ridiculous like, "Well, you never loved me," and the parent tries to say something really intelligent back to the kid to win the argument, who is in control of the conversation? The kid, right? When someone is latching onto being unreasonable with both hands and then wrapping their legs around it as well to hold on no matter what happens, you are not going to make them let go of their grasp with a little logic and wisdom. If you try, they have you beaten from the start. The way to success in such matters is to develop a very low IQ. Set your limits and then go brain dead. Leave them trying to figure things out. The results will be rewarding for everyone.

Now let's look at the specifics of Rule One in review:

RULE ONE
Adults set firm limits in loving ways without anger, lectures, threats, or repeated warnings.

- Adults set enforceable limits.
- Adults take care of themselves in loving ways by setting limits that say *what they will allow and what they will do.*
- Adults make their home resemble the real world as much as possible by letting natural consequences do the teaching rather than their edicts.

Love and Logic parents never rob their kids of significant learning opportunities by stepping in and taking responsibility for their kids' problems. Instead they apply the two rules of Love and Logic. It is now time for us to go on to the second rule and look at it in more detail.

CHAPTER THREE

Rule Two

As a review, the second rule of Love and Logic reads:

RULE TWO
When children cause problems, adults hand those problems back to them in loving ways.

What does this mean and how do we do it? Let me give you an example. Have you had a period of time in your house where you felt like whenever you tried to have a nice conversation with your spouse, your kids interrupted it with some sort of battle between them? Let's take a look at two different parents handling that same problem and see if we can find some clues about how to make our lives easier as we apply this second rule. Both of these parents have the same basic plan that my parents used with me when I was young; they are enforcing the very same logical consequence. Which one do you think will have the best result?

Now here's their plan: The parents are going to hire a babysitter—but they aren't going to say anything to the kids about it. Instead, they get ready to go out, and when the kids ask, "Where are you going?" they say, "We're going to go out on a date so we can have a conversation, since we are constantly interrupted at home. We have a babysitter coming to take care of you. Make sure you pay her. She said that she would take toys if you don't have any money."

Good example

..ow let's take a *closer* look at how the two different parents handled this situation.

Parent A

Parent A's kids see what is happening and ask, "Why are you getting dressed up? Where are we going?"

Parent A answers with anger, "Oh, we're going out on a date for crying out loud! We haven't had a chance to have a single conversation with each other in the last month! You guys are always starting fights and all that sort of thing to interfere. Well, we're getting sick and tired of it. Now, I hope you learn your lesson!"

The kids hear the doorbell. "Somebody's at the door."

Parent A responds sarcastically, "That's Mabel. She's going to be watching you, and she's going to ask you how you plan to pay her. I mean it! When we get back from this date, you guys better have a better attitude!"

Parent B

At Parent B's household, the kids see their parents getting dressed up and ask, "Where are we going?"

Parent B answers with sincere sadness, "Oh, we're going out on a date."

With a twinge of excitement the kids ask, "Well, where are we going to have the date?"

Parent B looks at them sadly and says, "Oh, this is such a bummer."

"What's a bummer?" the kids respond.

"It's a sad thing," Parent B answers matter-of-factly.

Then the doorbell rings. "Well, who's at the door?" the kids want to know.

With great empathy Parent B continues, "Oh, that's Mabel."

"Why is she here?"

"She's going to be your babysitter."

"But we don't want to stay with her."

"I don't blame you."

"Why are you guys going without us?"

"Well," Parent B answers soulfully, "the sad thing is that every time your mom and I try to talk, we get interrupted by you and your brother having problems. We sure do love you guys and would love to take you along, but we've got to get our talking done, too, and this way we can. So we'll see you when we get back." Then, matter-of-factly again, "Oh, and by the way, since we had to get Mabel to come because you keep interrupting us, you will need to pay her."

"But we don't have any money!"

"Not a problem. Mabel takes toys for payment. Hang in there. See you when we get home. We love you!"

Who *Really* Handed the Problem Back to Their Kids?

Now, let's take a look at these two different parents, and answer some questions.

1. Which kids are more angry, those of Parent A or Parent B?
2. Which kids are more confused? What I mean is, which kids are having to think the hardest?
3. Which kids are more resentful?
4. Which kids are more remorseful?
5. Which kids are going to maybe, just maybe, be more likely to put their parents in a nice clean nursing home someday?
6. Which kids are thinking, "What's their problem?"
7. Which kids are thinking, "Dang, now, we've got a problem"?
8. And, last but not least, which parent actually handed the problem back to the kids?

1. Parent A, 2. Parent B, 3. Parent A, 4. Parent B, 5. Parent B, 6. Parent A, 7. Parent B, 8. Parent B.

That's right, Parent B was the Love and Logic parent who actually handed the problem back to the kids. Parent A, on the other hand, never let go of the problem, even though he enforced the very same consequences.

Nearly thirty years ago we discovered that really effective parents and teachers always put the problem back in the kid's court *by using a strong dose of genuine empathy* before they deliver consequences. Too many parents are afraid to enforce the limits they set because *it hurts them too much. That is, they feel like they are playing the bad guy.* However, we need to realize that it is good guys who enforce rules and bad guys who let things slip. Empathy allows us to hold our kids firmly accountable without feeling like we are mean. It allows us to discipline them without losing their love.

Love and Logic parents and teachers always put the problem back in the kid's court by using a strong dose of genuine empathy before they deliver consequences.

If we have to take something away from our kids because they have misbehaved, we shouldn't feel bad for them, we should feel *sad for them.* Showing that sadness to our kids will help them understand that we had other desires for them, but because we love them and don't want to lie to them, we will do what we say even though it hurts. And remember, enforcing consequences when kids are young is much easier than it will be later in life when the stakes are higher, so stick to your standards. Let me give you a few examples.

Examples of Love and Logic's "Empathy-Consequence" Formula

Two brothers came to their father and asked, "Dad, where's our X-Box?"

"Oh dang," the father responds sadly, "you know I just got to noticing something. Every time you two played with that, you started fighting. And I just got to thinking how sad that would be if my kids were fighting over something that was just made out of a bunch of wires and circuit boards and stuff like that. So now, we're not going to have to worry about that. I gave it to charity."

Now I know what you are probably thinking. You paid good money for that X-Box, why would you give it away? I've actually had people say to me, "Wait a second. I'm not going to do that. If I spent all that money for something, I could never do that." Wiser parents understand that they must get rid of things like this *to save money*—and their kid's sense of responsibility. I can promise you that such a lesson will stick with your kids a lifetime and save you from spending thousands of dollars on therapy down the road, or from the medical treatment for your ulcer from putting up with fighting kids all of the time. Don't you think such a valuable learning experience is worth the cost of a game console?

I have noticed something else interesting as well. Parents who have the nerve and wisdom to do something like this gain a brand new status with their kids. Suddenly their words are respected like never before. A new confidence and authority oozes out of them that gets their kids' attention. Parents who have the strength to back up their words even when it means doing something like this have kids who are far less likely to test them in the future. In other words, I've found that parents who are willing to do business rarely *have to* do business.

> *Parents who have the nerve and wisdom to take expensive things away from their kids gain a brand new status with their kids. Suddenly their words are respected like never before.*

Let's take a look at another example.

A daughter comes to her mother and says, "Mom, would you take me over to Jesse's house?"

With sincere empathy, she answers, "Oh, that's never good."

"What?"

"Oh, I'd love to take you over to Jesse's, but there's a big problem."

"Well, what's the problem?"

By the way, the people who are really successful with this slow things way down. The faster their kids talk, the slower they do. So, slowly, the mom answers, "Oh, well, I'd love to take you over to Jesse's house, but the problem is this: I've been listening to so much bickering and arguing today that I don't think I have enough energy to drive. I am just so exhausted, I don't think it would be safe."

Another family was just finishing a vacation to Disney World and the two boys—Jake, who was eight, and Sam, who was ten—usually wrestled and tussled a good part of the time over the smallest of things but had been good as gold the entire trip. However, now that it was time to go home and they thought they had nothing further to behave for, the two fell to pushing and shoving again before the family was even out of the hotel. As Dad was paying the bill, Jake caught Sam off guard and knocked him into a side table near one of the couches and sent one of the lamps crashing to the ground and into a thousand different pieces.

Dad sighed, looking at the clerk. "I'm sorry," he said. "Please find out how much it will cost to replace and put it on our bill."

When they got outside, he told his boys, "You know, I am too upset about this to think clearly right now. We will talk about it when we get home." It was a quiet trip the rest of the way and both parents were at a loss about what to do about it.

Shortly after they arrived home, the hotel bill for the lamp came in the mail. $150! Mom and Dad discussed it and came up with the solution. When the kids got home from school that day they called them in. "Boys, we did the responsible thing with that hotel and paid for that lamp. As your parents, we have to take responsibility for our family, but we didn't break that lamp, you boys did. Since we love you, we paid the hotel the extra money. However, you boys will need to pay us back for it."

They gulped. "How much was it?"

"$150."

"But we don't have any money! How are we supposed to pay for something like that! We don't have jobs and our allowance isn't that much."

"Yeah," their dad conceded, "it certainly won't be easy or quick, but I know you boys can do it. You know, fall is coming up, and a lot of neighbors will need help raking their yards. I bet you could make $5 or $6 an hour doing that. I am sure we have some odd jobs around the house I don't want to do that I can pay you for as well.

You could also go into your room and collect some of your stuff and have a yard sale to raise part of the money. You guys are pretty smart; I know you can figure it out."

Over the next couple of months between the work that they did and deductions from their allowances, the two boys earned enough to reimburse their parents for the broken lamp. But that wasn't the best part. In doing so, the boys not only learned a valuable lesson about the consequences of their actions, but also that they were capable young men. When the debt was finally paid off, they both had a tremendous sense of accomplishment as a reward for having taken responsibility for their actions.

You see the pattern? Empathy, then consequence. And again, the parent is not telling the child what to do, only controlling what he or she will or won't do.

Now, if you can't think of anything else, blaming your inability to do something on the energy that has been sapped out of you by your kids' squabbles is a great catch-all. Let me give you another example.

"Mom, where's dinner?"

"Oh, no," Mom replies sadly, "I'm so worn out dealing with all this stuff."

"What stuff?"

"Oh, the stuff between you and your sister. All I had energy to do was open up a can."

She pointed to the table. There sat the contents of a can of Spam that seemed to glitter slightly as its gelatin caught the light. It was a sight to behold, as were the faces of her kids.

She certainly got their attention. By the way, at the Love and Logic Institute, we've learned that Spam can be an incredibly powerful behavior management tool. Once again, the war was won with that wonderful little can of good eats!

Keeping It Real

Why empathy? Listed below are some benefits of empathy over anger:

Chart

ny	Anger
Hands the problem back	Gives our kids an opportunity to blame us for the problem
Keep's the child's problem the "bad guy"	Makes us the "bad guy"
Creates responsibility	Creates resentment
Leaves us calmer	Leaves us more uptight
Helps kids calm down so that they can think	Revs kids up so they can fight
Teaches self-control	Teaches anger is the way to address problems
Leaves us feeling proud of ourselves	Leaves us feeling guilty

Yep, empathy allows our kids to think more about their own poor decisions than how mad we are at them and they are at us. In other words, the empathy allows their poor decision to be the bad guy while keeping us the good guys. It focuses the attention on their actions, right where it should be.

If you're thinking, "Yeah right, that sounds really simple and natural"; if you have your doubts, you're not alone. During a presentation to an audience in South Carolina a woman interrupted me at this point in my talk to say, "Ain't natural."

I said, "Really?"

She responded, "That's right! It ain't natural to be so nice to a kid who acts up like that." She went on, "I'll tell you what I say. I say, 'Young un, I brought you into this world, and I can take you out. When Momma ain't happy, ain't nobody gonna be happy.'"

And you know, she was right—I don't mean about the taking her kids out part; we don't condone that—but she was right that expressing empathy for kids who misbehave isn't natural. It is something we have to practice.

> *Don't use empathy when you're angry.*
> *Delay the consequence instead.*

So here are two down-to-earth practical ways to make showing empathy natural. The first one is this:

> *Don't use empathy when you're angry.*
> *Delay the consequence instead.*

Few people can be genuinely empathetic when they're angry, so don't even try. For most folks, their empathy sounds more like sarcasm under such circumstances. Instead, experiment with saying the following: "I am so angry right now, I can't even think straight. I haven't been this mad in a long time. I'm going to have to do something about this, but not now—I make better decisions when I'm calm. We'll talk later. Try not to worry about it."

I want to say this loud and clear. It's okay to be angry with your kids. It's normal. And it's okay for them to hear that you're angry with them. But they also need to see that you can handle that anger without losing control, making threats, or putting them down.

Some people get the wrong idea about Love and Logic because they think we are telling them to be artificially nicey-nicey to their kids all of the time. They think we are saying that the harshest thing a parent should ever say to a kid is, "Oh, this is so sad." But that is not what we are saying—to be like that isn't good for kids.

If kids never experience some well-handled anger from their parents when they are growing up, what are they going to do when they go to work and their boss yells at them? Probably melt into a puddle of goo on the floor. From time to time, our kids need to see us getting upset and handling it by calming down before dealing with the problem. Your kids need to see you do this so that they will know how to do this when they are angry. And yes! It's also okay to put dealing with the problem off until you can be more rational about it and have a plan for addressing it.

> *Parents provide a wonderful lesson
> when they are able to master their emotions.
> Kids will learn more from watching parents
> deal with life on a daily basis than
> they ever will from lectures.*

By the way, do you think the world would be a safer place if kids were seeing this modeled in their homes? I do. Kids need to see that anger isn't all-powerful. Parents provide a wonderful lesson when they are able to master their emotions. Kids will learn more from watching parents deal with life on a daily basis than they ever will from lectures. The power of modeling is truly amazing.

Every Time We Use Empathy, We Teach Empathy

A woman once told me this little story about her four-year-old son. She said, "Oh, I was constantly having to say to him things like, 'I'll be happy to play with you when you can be nice.' I even taught his siblings to say that to him because he had this habit of getting rough and throwing things around when he played with them. So the whole family was real good with the enforceable statements, 'We'll play with you when you can be nice,' or 'When you can be sweeter, we'll play with you,' or 'We will play with you when you can be nicer to our stuff.'"

Well, this little guy had a friend over, and she heard a commotion in his room. She ran to see what had happened, but before going in, she decided to just have a peek and see if she needed to intervene or not. So she peeked around the door jam, and she saw her precious four-year-old take his hat off and put in on the carpet, then he scooped all of his little matchbox cars and put them in his hat. He stood up, walked away from his friend, and said, "I'll play with you when you can be nice to my toys."

It was right then and there she thought to herself, "There's hope for this kid."

One Magic Phrase

The second way we make empathy more natural is to *find one empathetic statement you can use for any situation, then practice it over and over again.* Don't give in to the temptation to get creative and try to use more than one. Just pick one that fits you and stick to it.

> *Find one empathetic statement you can use for any situation, then practice it over and over again.*

Different phrases work for different dialects and cultures in different parts of the country. The key is to pick one that sounds natural for you. I was raised with, "What a bummer"—it got to the point where I could see a bummer coming when I was a kid—but that won't work for everyone. (By the way, you know I was raised with this Love and Logic stuff, right? I think that's why I became a psychologist. I had to figure out what happened to me when I was a child.)

Now for me "What a bummer" is too dated. It is too 1970s, or maybe even too late 1960s. However, if it works for you, great—whatever floats your boat. It just seems a bit too "groovy" or "far out" to me. The key is to find one little empathetic statement that gets you started. Once it comes out of your mouth, you have time to remember the other things you want to say.

Up in Minnesota I have a good friend who's a middle school principal. He likes to say, "Oh, that's never good." Down in South Carolina where I went to graduate school, some women would just say the kid's name about three million times really sadly. "Oh, Tommy, Tommy, Tommy. …" Or on a good day they might say, "Bless your heart."

I bumped into a guy in Omaha, Nebraska, who ran a residential treatment center. When he walked up to me during a conference, I couldn't see him at first because his belt buckle was so big. It was shiny with a steer on it. He also had a huge cowboy hat. He told me about his work, so I asked, "What's your empathetic statement?" He said, "Well, the first thing I do is I get them kids outside, then I kick the dirt real sad like. I tell you I kick that dirt and them kids know something bad's going to happen. Then I says this, 'Dang.'" I waited, but that was it: "Dang." Apparently it worked quite well for him.

Southern California I imagine you could just say, "Dude," and draw it out very long and sorrowfully.

I ran into a guy in Philadelphia who told me, "I can't do it."

"Can't do what?" I asked.

He said, "I can't do the empathy."

I said, "I bet you can do it."

He answered, "No, I can't do it."

So, being a smart aleck, I asked, "Okay, so what can you do?"

He thought for a moment, then said, "Well, my grandma, she had one."

"Okay, what did she say?"

"Well, when we'd act up, she'd look at us and go, 'Ohhhhhh,' in a long drawn out groan.'"

"Okay," I said, "that works for me!"

Whatever you choose doesn't have to be anything complicated. Some people like, "How sad." Other people like, "Oh man." Just find something you can say as a trigger phrase to remind you to show empathy for the mess your kids just created. I've compiled some classic favorites below. Maybe you have a unique one of your own. Remember, the way we say our phrase is just as important as the phrase itself. Words spoken with anger or sarcasm will drive a large and long-lasting wedge between us and our kids—make sure your words reflect the empathy of how sad you are for them instead.

What's Your Empathetic Phrase?

How sad.
Dang.
This stinks.
What a bummer.
I hate it when that happens.
Oh, man.
Ohhhhh.
That's never good.
Dude.
Bless your heart.
Oh, honey.

_____ (Fill in your own)

Ingrain It into Your Brain

Once you have your phrase, it's wise to burn it into your subconscious as the first thing that pops out of your mouth in any situation. Go down to the office supply store, get a whole stack of sticky pad notes, and on every single one of them write your empathetic statement. Let's say your empathetic statement is, "Oh, that's never good." So the first one will read, "Oh, that's never good." The second one will read, "Oh, that's never good." Then the next one will read, "Oh, that's never good." Got the idea?

> *Burn your empathetic statement into your subconscious as the first thing that pops out of your mouth in any situation.*

Then post these notes all over the house. When you wake up to the blaring of the alarm clock, as you reach over to turn it off, you see, "Oh, that's never good." You get up and go into the bathroom, and there on the mirror it says, "Oh, that's never good." You lift up the toilet seat, "Oh, that's never good." Your kid comes out of his room and on his forehead is a sticky note saying, "Oh, that's never good." You get in your car and on the dashboard you read, "Oh, that's never good." It takes a lot of repetition, but eventually you will get it. Then, when something happens with your kids, the first thing that will come to mind is, "Oh, that's never good."

Why go to such lengths? Because empathy is not a natural reaction to kids that are giving you brain damage. Habit is ingrained in the pathway responses of our brains—sort of like how rivers cut their way through valleys and create canyons. Research tells us that what we learn we never completely forget. We can't stop the water from flowing. If we want to change its course, we have to redirect it. In truth, we can't really break a habit—what we have to do is replace it with a better habit. This is a process that happens one choice and experience at a time.

If you were raised with parents whose first response to your misbehavior was to get angry and yell, chances are that this will be your first reaction as well. The two rules of Love and Logic are as important for setting the right response patterns for kids as they are in helping them think about solving their own problems. If anger is st instinct, then we will have to do some significant work to cnange it. It is why we make the sticky notes and put them everywhere—that empathetic statement becomes a signal for us to take a breath and redirect our energy away from anger to feeling empathy for our kids. It is why we tell our children, "I am too angry to deal with this right now. Let's talk about it later. Try not to worry."

It's like a tool shed. We tend to use the tool we have closest at hand to address whatever problem we are facing. If the only tool we have is a hammer, every problem looks like a nail. If whenever we face an issue with our kids we go into the tool shed and the first tool we find is anger, than that is the one we will use almost exclusively. Empathy is buried way back in the tool shed, so we have to make a conscious effort when we are not in a crisis to place it closer to the front. We're also wise to make sure that it's well-oiled and in proper working condition. We achieve this by practicing with it when we are not facing a kid-created problem—so when such a problem erupts the first thing to come out of our mouth is "Oh, that's never good," and not something else. In doing so, we start to change that old habit pattern one step at a time.

Handing Problems Back—In a Loving Way

Empathy is the key to rule two of Love and Logic. For review, here it is again:

RULE TWO

When children misbehave and cause problems, adults hand these problems back in loving ways.

- Adults understand that lessons learned from small mistakes early in life are far more affordable than large mistakes made later in life.
- Adults remember to provide strong doses of empathy before providing consequences.
- Children are given the gift of owning and solving their problems.

Although using empathy may feel strange or phony at first, it's by far the most powerful skill known to humanity for bringing the best out of others. Believe it or not, it even works on spouses! When we combine it with solid limits and logical consequences we have a powerful formula for effectively handling almost every parenting challenge we will face. This formula represents the basic bedrock foundation of Love and Logic. In the pages that follow, I'll build on this foundation by giving specific, step-by-step instructions for turning sibling spats into learning opportunities for your kids. I'll also provide more tips for staying sane even when your kids are acting crazy.

CHAPTER FOUR

How to End the War Between Your Kids

During one of my presentations on the basics of Love and Logic, a guy raised his hand and said, "Hey, wait a second. This all makes sense. We've taken the Love and Logic class before, so we understand these principles, but tell us what to do when the rubber hits the pavement. What do we do when our kids start bickering and battling or they start getting physical with each other?" In response, I gave him four specific steps he could take when his kids started going at it with each other. In the remainder of this book, I'll provide these steps—as well as plenty of practical examples.

Before I do, let's address a common question. A lot of people ask if these steps are age specific, and my response is "No." Certainly, we're going to talk a little bit differently to a kid who's two or three as opposed to one that is fourteen or fifteen or twenty, but these basic principles apply across the board. In fact, these basic concepts work in managing bickering adults as well. Before I go into each in greater deal, I'll list them below:

Step One: If you can do so without any major property damage or physical harm—stay out of it.

Step Two: Apply the Two Rules of Love and Logic.

Step Three: Expect them to solve their problem or go their separate ways.

45

Step Four: If they refuse to solve their problem, and it becomes your problem, let empathy and logical consequences do the teaching.

Now, let's look at each of those in more detail.

Step One: Stay Out of It

When I say, *stay out of it*, I mean avoid trying to figure out who started it—not that you ever really could anyway. I know parents who feel the urge to be Sherlock Holmes. The problem is that you never get enough clues to figure it out, and kids are really good at establishing just enough reasonable doubt that they can squirm out of anything. That's why you're far better off resisting the urge to search for clues to every unsolvable "whodunit."

Secondly, I recommend against trying to force any apologies. How many times have parents tried that and gotten responses that were anything but sincere?

Thirdly, be very reluctant to punish the kid who seems to be the bully. Now, why do I say that? It's not because I don't believe in justice. It's because two roles are being played here and neither one of them is healthy. One role, of course, is the bully or the aggressor; the other is the victim. You certainly don't want your kids growing up being professional victims—we have enough of those in our culture already—nor do you want your kids growing up being professional bullies—we also have enough of those.

So, here's the problem: when I try to punish one role, I run the great risk of rewarding the other. If I punish the aggressor all of the time, I teach the other that playing the victim is the way to get Mom and Dad's sympathy—and their sibling punished. Suddenly when that child is bored, he or she will start to pick at the other. Then when a fight erupts, it's far too easy for the child to become a "provocative victim." This child develops the habit of egging or "provoking" the other until he or she strikes back. The "aggressor" gets in trouble every time. Then the victim sits back and laughs, thinking, "Look at that! Being a victim really pays off." The best way to discourage the development of this unhealthy pattern is to resist the urge to punish the kid who seems to be the aggressor. In most cases it's wiser to hold both kids equally responsible for ending the strife.

> *You have to hold both kids equally responsible*
> *for ending the strife. Don't let them fall into*
> *the set roles of "bully" and "victim."*

The goal of staying out of it is to avoid teaching your kids that their bickering and fighting with each other is a good way to get your attention and change the color of your face. That's one of the main reasons kids go to battle with each other. I can prove it to you. When do kids tend to have the most trouble with each other? When you're on the phone, right? Or how about when you're trying to have a conversation with your spouse, or trying to answer some e-mails for work, or trying to drive? It's almost always some time when they don't feel like they are getting enough attention or piz-zazz out of you.

Since many children start sibling spats in an attempt to get the attention they crave, here's a little technique to prevent some of them: At least once a day, go to each of your kids and notice some-thing very specific about them, and do this only when they're behaving. You say—and the words are important—"I noticed . . ." and you describe one little thing about the kid that is positive. Examples include:

"I noticed that you like to draw."
"I noticed that you like to practice your jump shot."
"I noticed that you like to wash the car."
"I noticed that your friends really look up to you."
"I noticed that you've been riding your bike a lot."

Important!
Don't do this when the other kids are around. Just keep it between you and that child.

With little kids, noticing their shoes can be extremely effective. In fact, if you say to a little kid, "I noticed you have shoes," they tend to hold them up. Another thing that works well with little kids is noticing band-aids or wounds. "Wow. I notice that you have a big owie." (This also works on building relationships with adult or teenage males as well.) You might say, "I noticed you've grown about an inch." "I noticed that you're really into basketball right now." "I noticed that you got back on your bike when you fell off." Just notice something about them that would seem to have some meaning to them.

"I noticed _____." is all we say. We don't say, "That's great." Successful parents avoid praise under these circumstances. Why? Because it sounds phony. It sounds too corny. Instead, they just say, "I noticed. . . " and leave it at that. If our kids are teens, they will likely look at us sort of strange and say, "Huh? What?" All we say is, "Oh, I just noticed that." Then we walk away so that they don't feel too weirded out.

> *You just say, "I noticed _____." and leave it at that.*

Do this at least once a day when they are behaving and here's what you're going to find. Your kids will spend less time fighting with each other to get your attention. Your kids will also be less likely to argue and get defiant with you when you ask them to do things for you. Why will this be the case? Simply because there will never, ever be enough rewards or consequences to get kids to behave if we don't have a good, solid relationship with our kids in the first place. I know—being a busy, busy person myself—it is so easy to go through life and not even notice what's happening around you. I've been guilty of that. Sometimes I wake up and I realize my life is just a blur and I haven't noticed the beautiful things in my home like my children and my wife. It takes a little extra effort to build and maintain these relationships, but the result is a far happier life all the way around!

Human beings have such a strong need to be noticed that if they can't get noticed in a positive way, they will find a negative way to get noticed. And in far too many really good families the kids realize that they get far more attention—albeit disapproving—w they're acting out than when they're behaving. So a simple rule of great parenting is when your kids are acting really sweet, they ought to get a whole lot of attention, and when they are acting not-so-sweet, they should get very, very little attention. This is another reason why we want to stay out of it whenever possible—we don't want to reinforce their negative behavior by giving it too much special attention.

> *Human beings have such a strong need to be noticed that if they can't get noticed in a positive way, they will find a negative way to get noticed.*

Step Two: Applying the Two Rules

Staying out of the battle doesn't mean that we do nothing. It just means that we don't steal learning opportunities from our kids by solving problems for them. It also means that we don't steal our own sanity by making their unhappiness and stress ours. What we can do is move on to step two by applying the two rules of Love and Logic. Although this might sound complicated, all that's required to apply these rules is the following sentence:

Guys, it looks like you have a problem that you need to solve.

Yep! It just takes one sentence. Let's say your kids are starting to act up in another room or the back seat of the car or wherever. It's time to say, "Wow, guys, looks like you have a problem that you need to solve."

Does that apply both rules of Love and Logic? What is the first rule again?

Set enforceable limits without anger, lectures, threats, or repeated warnings.

Does saying, "You guys have a problem that you need to solve" set a limit? Yeah, it subtly says, "I have noticed your conflict, and if you don't solve it, consequences will soon follow." And what's the second rule?

**When a kid causes a problem,
we hand the problem back in a loving way.**

Does saying, "You guys have a problem that you need to solve" apply this second rule? Of course, you are directly letting them know they have a problem to solve.

I also recommend adding,
"I'd like to help you guys by giving you some ideas, but I'm only willing to help as long as there are no problems."
And
"I'll be willing to help as long as one person talks at a time and your voices are calm."

With these short, sweet statements, we set a limit, hand the problem back to them in a loving way, and show empathy by offering to help. You see, when we do this, we're not just dumping the problem in our kids' laps, but we're holding them responsible for solving it and enabling them to solve it at the same time. It is a process they will learn from. When they get used to solving their sibling-related problems, our stress goes down—and they become far better prepared for the real world.

Love and Logic parents are always willing to stand side-by-side with their kids when their kids are solving problems or experiencing the consequences of their decisions. Love and Logic parents are great consultants, and great consultants do what? They offer ideas their clients couldn't come up with on their own. When we do this as parents, we offer suggestions to our children—then we help them explore the consequences that might result from each suggestion. After doing so, we let them own the problem by resisting the urge to tell them exactly what to do.

Love and Logic Consultant Parents

- Are quick to get involved if their children are in danger.

- Are slow to get too involved when their children are learning affordable life lessons.

- Stand beside their children when they are struggling with the consequences of their actions.

- Never stand between their children and the consequences of their actions.

- Give helpful suggestions for coping.

- Resist the urge to simply tell their kids how to solve their problems.

- Help their children explore the possible outcomes of each suggestion.

- Remember that kids learn important life lessons even when they don't solve their problems well.

The easy way to start this is to say, "Some kids decide to . . ." and then follow it with a suggestion. After each idea we provide, we can help them explore the possible consequences by asking, "How would that work for you?" This approach is non-threatening, leaves the ultimate decision in their court, and lets us present a solution that is acceptable to us.

So it might sound like this: "Some kids decide to hide the stuff that they don't want their brother playing with. How would that work for you?" Or "Some kids decide to go play with different things that they won't fight over, " or "Some kids decide to go their separate ways if the activity they are trying to share ends in fighting." Another might be, "Some kids decide to find a channel that they can watch together without fighting about it." Although they want to help, wise parents avoid getting pulled into endless consulting sessions by never giving more than two or three suggestions.

*, let's get real! What's really going to happen when you do
won't work! The kids will refuse to take your suggestion. I
can absolutely guarantee it. It's entirely possible that they will completely ignore you. Or they will get frustrated and spout something
like, "You don't care!"

Why do I suggest doing this anyway? There are a number
of reasons. First of all so you can go to bed at night and say to
yourself, "At least I offered them help." It's nice to avoid feeling
like the guilty party when you are a parent. That's important,
isn't it? I always look at it this way: I want to be able to go to bed
every night and lay my head on my pillow thinking, "I was a class
act. I offered help. I did my very best. I gave my fifty percent in
the situation." And by the way, when we're helping our kids solve
their problems, Love and Logic teaches that we should never give
more than fifty percent of the effort needed to solve the problem.
We should never, ever work harder on our kids' problems than
they do. Why? Because when we do, our children begin to believe
that it's the job of others to clean up all of their messes and rescue
them from all of their challenges. There's another reason: When
we work harder than our youngsters, it leaves us feeling exhausted
and resentful toward them.

....

*We should never, ever work harder
on our kids' problems
than they do.*

....

Love and Logic parents will always stand beside their kids when
dealing with hard times. We do love them, after all. We will offer
ideas. We will offer emotional support. As Love and Logic parents,
we'll always be there for our kids, but we will never, ever stand between our kids and their problems or their consequences. There's a
big difference between standing beside our kids, being supportive,
and standing between our kids and the lessons they need to learn.
Even though our gestures to help may fall upon deaf or angry ears
in the short term, providing them will eventually lead our kids to
respect our wisdom and learn to solve the problems they face.

Take heart and remember the following:

Children typically learn the importance
of solving their own problems ONLY after failing to do so
and experiencing the consequences.

Step Three: Expect Them to Solve It or Separate

Staying out of the conflict by providing consulting services rather than search and rescue aid is tough! In fact, it's so hard for many of us that we end up losing our nerve and jumping into the fray. It's the fear that one of them might really get hurt. That's what makes it hardest for most folks. Worrying that long-term damage might occur, it's extremely easy to jump in and make their problem ours.

What do you do if you really are sure that your kids are going to get hurt? You protect them at all costs. Please don't misunderstand what Love and Logic is all about. Love and Logic is only about allowing kids to make affordable mistakes, not ones that aren't affordable. So we protect our kids from each other if we have to, and if there are serious problems of this nature, we find professional help.

Love and Logic is only about allowing kids to make
affordable mistakes, not ones that aren't affordable.

However, in the ninety-five percent of families where the kids are healthy and the parents are healthy and all of the relationships are basically healthy, the best thing is to distance yourself from getting more than fifty percent involved. Your kids will be better for it. If you ask any therapist, most will give you the same advice. They will talk to you about how to fine-tune it to fit the particular nuances of your family, and how to protect the kids if things get too rough, but the bottom line is this:

If your kids know you will solve their problems,
then you will always have to solve their problems—they will never
grow to solve them on their own.

ere's another sad consequence of getting over-involved in our kid's conflicts: They begin to rely on our rescue rather than their own self-control. They actually get rougher with each other, because they know that we will save them from each other if things get out of control. Lonnie and her boys are a great example of this happening.

The Little First Aid Kit

I met Lonnie years ago, when her boys were teenagers. From day one when they were very little, she spent all of her energy trying to protect them from each other. Of course, the harder she worked at it, the rougher they got, and by the time they became teenagers, it was just awful. It was terrible. She kept asking herself, "Wait a second, I think we have a pretty healthy family. I am always there for the kids. So why is this such a problem?"

To understand it helps to go to the circus. Let's pretend it's the night before the opening performance and there's a couple of tightrope walkers practicing. Both of them are walking a thin wire. About 200 feet below one of them is a net, so if he falls off what happens? Right, he hits the net and he is fine. Beneath the other, however, even though he is on a line at the same height, there is no net or anything but hard concrete. If he falls off of the wire, it's not going to be pretty. Which tightrope walker is going to be paying the most attention to his next move? The one without the net!

What too often happens in good, healthy families is the parents have been over-involved in many of the issues between their kids—in essence, they have provided too many safety nets. They have spent all of their time rescuing their kids from problems. So, instead of having fewer problems, their kids have more. Why is this? Simply because these kids have come to believe that there will always be a safety net to catch them, no matter how careless they are. They start thinking to themselves, "Why do I have to be careful?" The problem is that some day their parents aren't going to be there to catch them.

When parents play the role of rescuer, what they really do is teach their kids to depend on being rescued. They come to rely on external safeguards rather than self-control. Look at our society as a whole right now. Do we too frequently rely on external safeguards rather than self-control? Is it just me, or are you also amazed by the silliness of many warning labels included on products? It's just a thought, but I believe our society today could greatly benefit from more people who can think for themselves, anticipate potential dangers, and exercise self-control.

And which do you want for your kids? Do you want them to be saying to themselves, "You know what? I don't need to worry that much about my next step because somebody is going to suddenly appear and make sure that nobody gets hurts," or do you want your kids thinking, "You know what? The quality of my life—in fact, the length of my life—depends heavily on every single decision I make because there may not be somebody there that can make everything okay if I mess up again"?

What we are learning from teachers, school administrators, police officers, and people who work in the juvenile courts is that more and more teenagers are doing horrible things. They violate the law in unbelievable ways. In Texas four sweet little teenage girls decided to rob convenience stores with a gun. These kids were good kids from basically good families. However, these sweet kids all got between seven and eight years in the federal pen—and when the sentences were read in that courtroom, the shock on their faces was amazing. They could not believe that those consequences were a result of their actions, because they weren't familiar with any uncomfortable consequences for any of their actions. When kids never understand there are consequences for their actions because they have been rescued all of their lives, very, very sad things can happen.

Lonnie's kids were in that same dilemma, because she had always rescued them. So rather than getting better, they got worse. They had it firmly locked into their heads that there was no need to worry about how rough they got with each other. They had learned that their mother would suddenly appear and break things up before things got too bad. Things were about to change. Mom had learned a little Love and Logic. She decided she'd back out a little bit. She started giving them more responsibility for solving their own problems.

What happens when we give people responsibility who aren't used to having responsibility? They're going to blow it. It's guaranteed. So when is it best for kids to blow it? When they are young, you are there to watch over them, and the stakes are low. Price tags on mistakes go up every day, so the sooner they learn the lesson that they are responsible for their own actions, the better.

What happens when we give people responsibility who aren't used to having responsibility? They're going to blow it. It's guaranteed.

So what happened with Lonnie's teenagers? Well, it got so rough in that home one day that one of them took the other and pushed him against the door jam and it dislocated his shoulder. Lonnie got both of them in the car, drove them down to the hospital, and let the medical staff handle it. She stayed calm, and she held her boys accountable for the accident. They paid for the gas that she burned up driving them to the hospital. They paid for the insurance co-pay. She also charged them for her time. There were a number of different consequences and she held them responsible for every one of them.

Now please, don't misunderstand me. I am not advocating letting kids hurt each other. Love and Logic does not preach that violence is the answer. We don't want kids to pummel each other so that they can learn their lessons. That's the last thing we want. But here's what I do want you to learn from Lonnie's story: *Our kids are far more likely to hurt each other when we overprotect them from the logical consequences of their bratty, nasty behavior when they are little. If we wait until they are teens to begin allowing them to be responsible for their actions, the consequences they will suffer will be far more painful.*

Love and Logic does not preach that violence is the answer.

The odds go way up that kids will hurt each other—or will get hurt—in this world by thinking, "I can be snotty and obnoxious to others, and I just know that my mother will somehow beam down out of the air and save me from being punched, stabbed, or shot." We all know that Mom's not showing up, and that kid is in for a painful awakening.

Now had Lonnie's story ended right there, I would have no reason for telling it to you, but it didn't. Lonnie was a creative mom with a sense of humor and she wanted to find a way of letting her boys solve their own problems without getting hurt again, so here is what she did. One day while she was walking down the aisle at Walgreens not long after this, she spied a cute little first aid kit. A light bulb went off over her head. So she bought the kit and took it home.

After that, anytime her kids started arguing with each other, she'd hand them the first aid kit and say, "Guys, maybe you want to save a little cash this time and do the repairs yourself instead of going to the hospital." That first aid kit became a fun little signal to the kids. Whenever they saw it, they'd think, "Maybe something bad could happen."

Soon it got to the point where that kit was starting to collect some dust because they had felt the financial pinch of roughhousing. Then it happened. Lonnie told me, "I got sucked into the worst argument I'd ever had with my older son. We were going at it. You see, he rolled his Jeep and then he wanted money to fix it, and I just couldn't help at that time. Besides, I told him, 'I'm not the Bank of Mom,' and I just got into it with him. Oh, it wasn't good.

"Then suddenly my younger son walked in and he's got the kit. He held it up and he said, 'Mom, maybe you and Ryan could save some money and—'"

She said, "I discovered something very precious at that moment: It is totally impossible to argue with somebody when you're laughing." Those boys still tease their mom about that, and now they're in their twenties.

So there is always hope for kids. Nevertheless, the older they get, the more mistakes will cost them. So isn't it better to let them suffer the relatively painless consequences as toddlers and grade schoolers than to wait until they are pushing each other through walls as teenagers or young adults?

Step Four: Let Empathy and Consequences Do the Teaching

If your kids continue to bicker and battle—despite your valiant attempts to guide them toward solving their disputes—then their problem becomes your problem. It's your problem because it hassles your ears, frays your nerves, and leaves you feeling exhausted. A critical concept understood by all wise Love and Logic parents is the importance of taking good care of ourselves and "handing the problem back" in a caring way. We do this by letting empathy and logical consequences do the teaching.

Sometimes this is easy. There are those rare occasions when a consequence just pops in your head, and you say to yourself, "That's going to work." For example, it's relatively easy when your kids are arguing and bickering over some item to simply remove the item. Or when your kids have been hassling you over their problems and then ask you to take them somewhere, it's pretty easy to say, "Oh, I'll be happy to drive you when I feel charged up rather than drained."

However, at other times it's not so simple. How often have you been at a complete loss for a logical—and legal—consequence? I ran into a lady who had this problem with her boys. She said, "I'd be taking them to town in the backseat of the car and it would become awful. It wasn't much of a problem when the weather was good and we weren't in a hurry, because I kept a lawn chair and a book in the trunk. Whenever it would get loud, I just pulled over, and I'd pop the trunk. I'd get my lawn chair out, set it up, and I'd read my book. I wouldn't say a word to them. I'd just read my book. When it quieted down, I'd get back in the car and drive. If they started up again, I'd pull over again, set up my lawn chair, and go back to my book."

She told me she had set up that lawn chair in some of the most amazing places: rural communities by the side of the road, McDonald's parking lots, you name it, she'd stopped there and read. Then she went on to ask me, "But what do you do when the weather's really bad, or you're in a hurry and you can't stop?"

I asked her to experiment with one of my very favorite Love and Logic techniques. One day they were driving down the road on the way to the doctor's office. Almost on cue, the kids started arguing

like crazy in the backseat. She had enough time to pull over qɪ
but that was it. So she slammed on the brakes, pulled over, and put
her hand up on her forehead. Then she moaned, "Ohhhhhh," and
slumped over the wheel.

The boys in the backseat jumped right on this, "What's wrong,
Mom? Are you okay?"

She answered, "Oh yeah, I'm okay. It's just that I'm really getting
my energy drained." Stunned, they quieted down, so after a bit, she
drove back on the road, and, sure enough, they started to bicker
and battle again.

Well, she couldn't pull over again, so from time to time she'd just
go "Ohhhhhh." This didn't change their behavior a bit during the
trip, but she didn't expect that it would. She was simply setting the
stage for later. Every time she moaned, "Ohhhhh," she reminded
herself that it's okay to let kids think they have gotten away with
something in the short term—if that'll buy you some time to figure
out how to handle it well in the long term.

....

> *It's okay to let kids think they have*
> *gotten away with something in the short term—*
> *if that'll buy you some time to figure out*
> *how to handle it well in the long term.*

....

Later that evening, she went to them and she said, "Guys, this is
such a bummer."

They said, "What, Mom?"

She said, "Do you know that when you argue and fight in the
backseat of the car that it drains my energy?"

Now, let me stop here and make a comment. Was this some kind of
crazy manipulation game she was playing? Was she making all of this
up? No, of course not, their fighting really was draining her energy.

What else drains your energy? How about when kids lie? Does
that drain your energy? How about when you don't know where your
kids are because they've stayed out too late and you're worried sick?
Does that drain your energy? Or how about when they don't do their
chores? Or when their eyeballs are always rolled up into their head

when you speak to them? Or when they're sassy and have an attitude all day—does that drain your energy? You bet it does.

I call this technique "the energy drain."
It is a generic consequence for when something
more fitting doesn't immediately occur to you.

I call this technique "the energy drain." It is a generic consequence for when something more fitting doesn't immediately occur to you. If you can't think of a more specific consequence, have an energy drain.

Here is how it works. Let's say your kids are hassling each other when you're on the phone. "Mommy, Tommy took my blah, blah, blah." You know what I mean. What do you do? The only thing you can do is maybe say a little, "Oohhhhh," but do your best to complete the call. (By the way, when your kids are hassling you and you're on the phone, continue the conversation even after the other person has hung up. Never let them cut your phone call short, because if you do, what do the kids realize? "I can get Mom or Dad off the phone quicker if I hassle them." So I recommend you just keep having the conversation until they finally leave you alone. Tell your kids, "Hey, guys, as soon as it gets quiet, I'm probably going to be able to wrap this up, but this could take days if not.") The goal at this point is to avoid giving them too much attention while they are making noise and yanking on your sleeves.

Later that day, go to them with great empathy and say, "Guys, do you know that when you interrupt me on the phone, it really drains my energy?" How will they respond? They'll probably look at you like you're from Mars and act very, very confused. Then, right in the middle of their perplexed look, ask, "So, how are you going to put that energy back?"

Then they'll look at you like you're from another universe. They'll shrug their shoulders and say, "I dunno."

Since they've admitted they don't know, it's time to go into consultant mode. Say, "Here's some ideas. Some kids decide to give their mother a glass of lemonade, but that's not all, they say,

'Mom, take this lemonade and lay down on the couch and get really comfortable because we have a lot of work to do.' Then they go in and get all the stuff out of their room, like their rollerblades and their iPods, and they put it all out on the lawn. Then they make a sign that says 'Sale,' and they sell all of that stuff so that they can buy their mom a gift certificate to the mall. Now, that would charge me up." (Here's another little hint. When you're offering suggestions for your kids to put energy back into you, start with an outrageous one. Of course we wouldn't really expect our kids to sell everything they have. The reason we offer this is to inject a little humor into the situation and to make the other more realistic alternatives look even better to them. There's another reason: Since kids tend to reject the first thing you say anyway, don't waste a good one.)

When you're offering suggestions for your kids to put energy back into you, start with an outrageous one. Why? Because it makes the next ideas look much better. And since kids tend to reject the first thing you say anyway, don't waste a good one.

You might even say something like this, "Some kids decide to sell an organ. You've got a couple kidneys—you only need one. Buy me a car. That would really charge me up." Make sure that you only use this sort of humor with kids who can understand it and won't take you seriously. Since most kids younger than ten or so often have trouble understanding this type of humor, it's usually wise to avoid it.

After Mom had gone through a couple of crazy ones, she said to her boys, "Some kids decide to clean up all of that dog doo-doo out in the yard. I'm not sure why, but when kids clean up dog doo-doo, it really charges me up." Another offer: "Some kids decided to collect some money and hire a babysitter so that their mom and dad can go out on a date. If I could go out with your dad and have some fun that would really put energy back into me."

Kids can replace their parents' energy in the following ways:

- Doing extra chores
- Staying home instead of being driven some place they want to go
- Paying for a babysitter so that Mom and Dad can get away for a while
- Making their parents proud by helping the neighbors, people at church, or others in the community

What do you think will probably happen when you apply this technique and ask your kids to replace your energy? They might just say, "That's dumb, Mom."

If that happens, reply calmly, "I know. But if you don't do something to put my energy back into me by such and such a time, I'm going to have to do something about it myself."

I have found that, "I'm going to have to do something," can be very effective. In fact, I've actually come to believe that "something" is the most dreaded consequence known to childkind. The beauty of it is that you don't have to know what that something is any more than they do. It just buys you time to calm down and think!

Do you remember the mother with the two backseat brawlers? She went through this entire routine and guess what happened? Absolutely nothing. They didn't even attempt to put energy back into her and that was a sad, sad thing—for them! When they came home from school the next day, they wanted to play some video games, but couldn't find their Nintendo. So they asked, "Mom, where's our Nintendo?"

She responded, "I learned something today."

They said, "What'd you learn, Mom—and where's our Nintendo?"

She replied, "I learned something. I learned that when I donate things to the church, it really charges me up."

The kids' jaws dropped. "You're not serious."

"Yes, I am."

"But you can't do that."

"But I already did."

How long do you think it took those boys to realize that it was always wiser to do a few extra things around the house and put energy back in their mom, than to wait and try to figure out what crazy "something" she was going to do next?

Mom admitted to me, "After that, my energy drains really evolved. They changed. The first ones were kind of sad, and I'd say, 'Ooh. Energy drain,' long and drawn out and filled with gloom. Then they started getting more happy and expectant. I'd be like, 'Ooh, goody! An energy drain.' Then pretty soon they got like this: 'Yesssss! Energy drain!' I would even throw in a fist pump." It didn't take her long to realize that every time her kids drained her energy, she had less housework to do.

But she went on to say, "Then something horrible happened. It was tragic. At the height of elation—things were going so well; I wasn't doing any housework; it was great. The world was wonderful. The sky was blue. Birds were tweeting. Then something horrible happened. They started arguing with each other. I thought to myself, 'Yes! Energy drain!' But before I could say anything I heard one of them say, 'Shut up, man.' And the other one said, 'Yeah, or we're going to have to do chores.' And then they were quiet."

She said, "That day I realized I was going to have to start doing my own housework again." Then she smiled.

Surprising Developments

When our kids bicker and battle around us and it becomes our problem, how do we hand that problem back? Do they need to do something to replace our energy? And how early can you start with the energy drain technique?

I know a woman who used it with a three-year-old. That little kid had found a "word." It wasn't a pleasant word. It wasn't even a rated "G"-rated word! Have you ever noticed that kids always learn those words at daycare or from the neighbor kids? They surely never hear those at home and certainly not from us. Well, the "word" was pretty troubling, and he used it with his sibling. The mom needed to nip that in the bud, so she started having these little energy drains, and he'd do different jobs around the house. One of his favorites was dusting. He put a lot of energy back into his mother through dusting. She'd put a sock on his hand and he'd just go around the house wiping dust off tables and shelves. She said, "Everything below my waist looked pretty good."

The technique was working well. Then when they were in the car one day driving along, she almost got run off the road on an interchange from one freeway onto another. Some crazy guy came whipping around her, and you know what? That word popped right out of her mouth. She sat there in good healthy parental denial. She told herself, "He couldn't have heard that. There's no way. I said it too softly."

Then she looked in the mirror, and her son was shaking his little finger at her, "Ooh, Mommy. Energy drain."

What do you say to a kid who's nailed you like that? Well, she just looked up in the mirror and said, "Honey, do you think an ice cream cone will put that energy back into you?"

He said, "Yeah, I think it'll help." So they went and got an ice cream and had a good time together.

From this story we can all learn that establishing loving discipline with our kids doesn't mean that we have to be mean—or that they will end up being angry at us forever. What it really means is that we are showing them that we truly love them enough to show them how to live respectful, responsible, and happy lives. Parents who are afraid to discipline their children in this way don't end up eating ice cream with them in the long run.

CHAPTER FIVE

Handling Battling Tots, Nitpicking Nuisances, Raging Teens, and Other Conflicts that Threaten Our Sanity

W hat's the main thing that I hope you get out of this book? I hope you learn how to give yourself a break. What do I mean by that? There are an awful lot of people who were raised to believe that "good mothers" and "good fathers" always make sure that their kids are happy—that "good mothers" and "good fathers" always make sure their kids are never inconvenienced or frustrated by things, or always make sure their kids have clean underwear on just in case they get in an accident. They believe that "good mothers" and "good fathers" always make sure that their kids play nicely with each other—and it is their job to make their kids love each other. This kind of thinking puts all the pressure on the parent and none on the kids to make themselves happy, to take care of themselves, to learn to get along with each other, or to learn how to live—and love—life. This turns moms and dads into thankless servants in their own households and turns their kids into tyrants. Yes! I want you to give yourself a break.

I wish I could teach you how to make your kids love each other. I wish that we had control over that, but we don't, do we? That's up to who? Them. There are some families where the kids have personalities just different enough that they never quite gel with each other. Is that anybody's fault? No. Absolutely not.

Ha-ha!

I know that some of you have kids who came out of the womb holding a dove, and in the dove's beak was an olive branch. Those are the kids who look at the world and say, "I'm here to help. Why can't we all just get along?" Then some of you—maybe even the next time around for the parents that had that first kid—had a child who came out of the womb smoking a cigar. That kid had little red boxing gloves on and looked at the doctor and said, "Ah, hold on a second there. Before you consummate this transaction by cutting that cord. Let's make sure we know who's in charge here, eh? Right? It's me." And that kid looked around and tried to figure out what other people wanted so he or she could do the exact opposite. That's one of the most powerful ironies of life, isn't it?

But such things need not cause us to pull our hair out, give us stomach ulcers, or send us to an early grave. Instead we can spin the hay and stubble of sibling rivalry into relationship gold by applying the simple techniques we explored in the last chapter. They let us turn frustration into fun and war zones into peaceful provinces. And don't be surprised if your kids accidentally grow closer in the process as well.

The Magic Touch

Also, don't feel tied to doing things exactly the same way as outlined here. Being a parent is part common sense, part creative genius. Putting your own individual, magic touch on these principles is the stuff of family lore. Your inspiring solutions will be the stuff of legend to your grandkids when your kids finally learn what they put you through. Hopefully your example will be a foundation for the great relationship they'll have with their kids.

Had any more thoughts about those three stories I shared in chapter one? While you may have come up with some great solutions of your own, here is how those parents solved them.

Patrice and Brett

You will probably remember Patrice, the seven-year-old image consultant, and her ten-year-old brother Brett, who never seemed to measure up to her expectations. When Brett met her disapproval, the entire house suffered because of the noise of her nitpicking and his retaliations.

So one night their father was watching TV and came across one of those reality shows where pixilated guys running around without shirts have encounters with law enforcement officers. Watching for a moment, he saw several troublemakers arrested and fined for disturbing the peace. This got him to thinking about real world consequences for his kids' constant violations of the peace in their home, so he had a talk with them. "You know having things quiet and peaceful in our house is something that is really important to your mom and I, and your squabbling with each other all the time really disturbs that peace. In the real world, when people disturb the peace of others, they are put in jail or fined. I would hate for either of you to end up like that, so I was thinking it would be a good idea if we started having fines for violations of the peace in our house."

Of course, his kids looked at him like he was nuts and went on without giving it another thought. He didn't let their "Sure, whatever," bother him, though. He had set an enforceable limit and done his part. Now it was time for them to do their part—challenge that limit. *always!*

So, a few days later, they got into another argument and the noise levels rose. Instead of getting angry with them, the dad told them, "Hey kids, it is getting a little loud in there. This is getting pretty close to being a violation of the peace. Maybe you guys should tone that down or separate from one another." And, of course, they ignored him, but he said nothing more.

At the end of the week, when the allowance envelopes were handed out, instead of the four dollar bills and two quarters they normally received, they got a little hand written note that said, "Citation for disturbing the Peace. Fine: $5."

"Hey, Dad, what's this?"

Their dad took the slip of paper the kids handed him and read it. "Oh, that's never good."

"What?" they asked.

Allowance?

"Well, this is a citation for disturbing the peace. Remember when I told you a couple of days ago that you were getting close to violating the peace of our home?"

"Yeah."

"Well, you did. You disturbed our peace, so this is the fine. Since it is also a little more than you usually get for your allowance, we will have to get the rest of it out of next week's allowance, so try not to worry about it. It shouldn't be a problem again."

And it wasn't. Anytime they started getting too loud, all he had to do was say, "Wow. It sounds like that might be another disturbance of the peace violation," and the kids would either separate or take the squabble elsewhere out of earshot, where they would have to solve the problem for themselves. Peace was restored and the two started doing a lot more thinking than their parents about solving their differences.

Lawrence and Robert

Little Lawrence and his twin brother Robert were too young to get an allowance, though, and when their parents started reading some of our Love and Logic materials and listening to some of the CDs, they felt most of the examples were too advanced for their two-year-olds. They understood the principle of "if you can't do the time, don't do the crime," but weren't sure how to make it relevant to their twins.

After one of my presentations, they came up and asked me what I thought, so I taught them the "Uh-oh!" song. They were thrilled, said they would use it the next time their kids started fighting, and that they would get back to me on the results. So they went home and got ready.

Sure enough, in a couple of days, Lawrence and Robert got into it again. So Mom came into the room and, in a sing-songy voice said, "Uh-oh! Looks like you guys need a little away time." Then she scooped up Lawrence and carried him into the twins' room—which she and her husband had made safe so he couldn't hurt himself by continuing his tantrum. As she gently placed him in the room, she replied with empathy, "I'll see you again when you are feeling sweeter." Without another word, she closed the door to let him know she expected him to stay put. Dad sat right outside in the hall, making certain that he was safe—and that he didn't make a jail break. Next, she headed back to apprehend Robert.

As she scooped him up he suddenly appeared very concerned about his brother—whom just seconds earlier he was pummeling. With one tiny little finger, he pointed at the door as they went by it, making concerned noises that couldn't quite form themselves into words. Then there, in the family room, was a crib where Robert could do his time and his own thinking without causing troubles for anyone else or hurting himself if he continued to rage.

When things were quiet, Mom came and got Lawrence, told him how much she loved him, gave him a kiss on the head and carried him out of his room. Then she went and got Robert with the same love and rejoined the brothers.

It didn't take them too many more trips before they understood that it was better to play together nicely than do time for fighting. Yes, before long all they needed to hear was "Uh-oh" and they quickly transformed from hissing wildcats into gentle bunnies. It was a system that returned peace to the home quickly and fit the age and infractions of the twins.

Jake and Sam

Of course, Jake and Sam, the teenage brothers, were far too big for the "Uh-oh!" song. Over the years the two had learned they were oil and vinegar and found that the best way to live life was separately. It was a sad thing for brothers to be so different genetically, but it is more common than most parents realize. Sometimes kids are just different from birth, and the best thing is to let them figure out how to get along on their own terms.

When they had to go somewhere together in the car, there was no way for them to avoid each other, and before their mom hardly got out of the driveway, they were already bickering and battling. This wore their mom's nerves thin in no time. Since she had been listening to some Love and Logic CDs in the car, she was determined not to fight with them, but in the heat of the moment, she wasn't sure what to do. So, almost out of impulse looking for an answer, she took one of my dad's Love and Logic presentations and slipped it into the CD player.

As Jim Fay's voice filled the car, a stunned silence settled in the back seat. Then, "Ah, Mom! Why did you put that in! We hate listening to this! Take it out!"

The effect amazed her and she thought about it for a moment as the two complained and pleaded, but also stopped fighting. Finally, she said, "I'm sorry guys, but when you two fight like that, I realize that I need to get better at this Love and Logic stuff. So whenever you guys fight, it reminds me that I need to listen to these CDs again. Please bear with me. I just want to be the best mom I can for you both."

It is the most direct application of Love and Logic I have ever heard. I wouldn't be surprised if those two had those lessons memorized before they figured out they didn't have to fight every time they went somewhere.

The Most Important Factor

Before we finish, I want to discuss a common misconception about Love and Logic I have heard as I travel and speak with parents and teachers. While Love and Logic is here to make your life better and help you take really good care of yourself, Love and Logic is not a way for you to "get your kids out of your hair" as a rule, or reduce the amount of time you have to deal with your kids. Sometimes, especially in our books, it seems easy to hear the emphasis we put on setting limits and letting consequences do the teaching and miss the emphasis we put on these techniques as a way for you to be on the same side as your kids and end the fighting, anger, and lectures. Love and Logic is there to eliminate one of the most painful aspects of being a parent—disciplining your children for their misbehavior—and the things that cause the most distance and friction between parents and children—the nagging, lectures, and anger.

While the techniques and principles of Love and Logic can improve your relationship with your kids, they can't replace that relationship. If you are normally antagonistic and sarcastic with your children, Love and Logic won't work for you until you can eliminate those tones of voice and that body language from your communication with your kids. Empathy is hard to fake. You can use the same words we have used here and get negative results because the empathy is just not there. If you are angry every time you speak with your kids, these techniques will likely backfire. If this is what you are experiencing, it is not time to buy a different line of parenting books, but to go to someone in your community who specializes in family counseling and get help.

After all, while these techniques and principles can help every parent-child relationship, it is up to us as the parents to figure out the best way to apply them. We still have to know the unique needs and characteristics of each of our kids and be creative in how we relate to them and love them. Nothing in the universe can replace that spark of the divine that exists when you are together with your family and you are seeing that the fruits of your labor are making it more peaceful.

Love and Logic does not teach you how to be a good parent. Most of the parents I meet are already good parents. The principles it teaches are to give you more room to be a good parent and take the "good parent, bad parent" routine out of your daily interactions with your kids. It is about taking better care of yourself so that you have more energy for the fun parts of being a parent and spend less energy on the frustrating parts. It is about giving you better tools to parent so that you can release better kids into the world.

Love and Logic is about making it easier to love your kids and helping them better understand the connection between their decisions and the consequences of those decisions. Thanks for all of your diligent efforts in that regard. I know you wouldn't have invested the time to read this book if you weren't already a great parent.

Keep up the good work!